HAL LEONARD GUITAR METHOD BOOK 1

SECOND EDITION

BY WILL SCHMID AND GREG KOCH

ISBN 0-7935-1245-X

HAL•LEONARD® CORPORATION

7777 W. BLUEMOUND RD. P.O. BOX 13819 MILWAUKEE, WI 53213

W9-BSO-288

Visit Hal Leonard Online at
www.halleonard.com

YOUR GUITAR

This book is designed for use with any type of guitar—acoustic steel-string, nylon-string classical, or electric. Any of these guitars can be adapted for use in a wide variety of styles of music.

STEEL-STRING

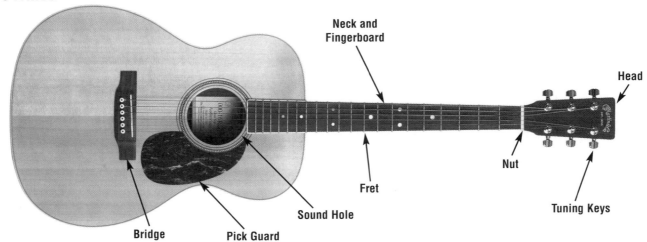

NYLON-STRING

ELECTRIC

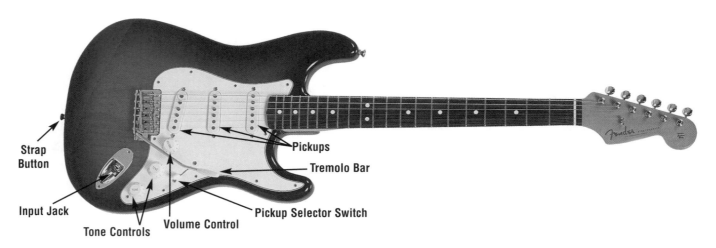

If you are using a solidbody-electric or an acoustic-electric be sure to practice with an amplifier some of the time.

TUNING

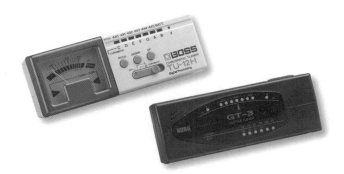

Tuning Keys

When you are tuning your guitar, you will adjust the pitch (highness or lowness of sound) of each string by turning the corresponding tuning key. Tightening a string raises the pitch and loosening it lowers the pitch.

The strings are numbered 1 through 6 beginning with the thinnest string, the one closest to your knee. Follow the instructions below to tune each string in sequence, beginning with the sixth string.

TUNING WITH AN ELECTRONIC TUNER

An electronic tuner "reads" the pitch of a sound and tells you whether or not the pitch is correct. Until your ear is well trained in hearing pitches, this can be a much more accurate way to tune. There are many different types of tuners available, and each one will come with more detailed instructions for its use.

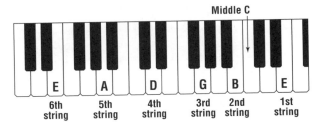

TUNING TO A KEYBOARD

If you have a piano or electric keyboard nearby, play the correct key (see diagram) and slowly turn the corresponding tuning key until the sound of the string matches the sound of the keyboard.

Middle C

E	A	D	G	B	E
6th string	5th string	4th string	3rd string	2nd string	1st string

ANOTHER WAY TO TUNE

To check or correct your tuning when no pitch source is available, follow these steps:
- Assume that the sixth string is tuned correctly to E.
- Press the sixth string at the 5th fret. This is the pitch A to which you tune your open fifth string. Play the depressed sixth string and the fifth string with your thumb. When the two sounds match, you are in tune.
- Press the fifth string at the 5th fret and tune the open fourth string to it. Follow the same procedure that you did on the fifth and sixth strings.
- Press the fourth string at the 5th fret and tune the open third string to it.
- To tune the second string, press the third string at the 4th fret and tune the open second string to it.
- Press the second string at the 5th fret and tune the first string to it.

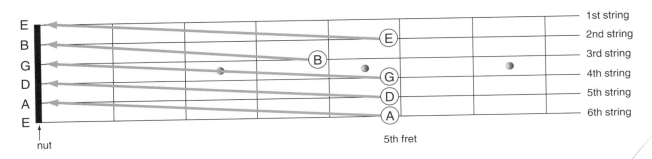

This is called **relative tuning** because the strings are tuned relative to one another.

PLAYING POSITION

There are several ways to hold the guitar comfortably. On the left is a typical seated position, and on the right is the standing position. Make sure you practice sitting and standing. Observe the following general guidelines in forming your playing posture:

- Position your body, arms, and legs in such a way that you avoid tension.

- If you feel tension creeping into your playing, you probably need to reassess your position.

- Tilt the neck upwards—never down.

- Keep the body of the guitar as vertical as possible. Avoid slanting the top of the guitar so that you can see better. Balance your weight evenly from left to right. Sit straight (but not rigid).

Left-hand fingers are numbered 1 through 4 (Pianists: Note that the thumb is not number 1.) Place the thumb in back of the neck roughly opposite the 2nd finger. Avoid gripping the neck like a baseball bat with the palm touching the back of the neck.

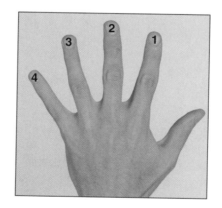

These photos show the position for holding a pick and the right-hand position in relationship to the strings. Strive for finger efficiency and relaxation in your playing.

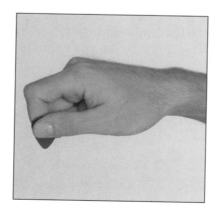

MUSICAL SYMBOLS

Music is written in **notes** on a **staff**. The staff has five lines and four spaces between the lines. Where a note is written on the staff determines its **pitch** (highness or lowness). At the beginning of the staff is a **clef sign**. Guitar music is written in the treble clef.

STAFF

TREBLE CLEF

Each line and space of the staff has a letter name. The **lines** are, (from bottom to top) E - G - B - D - F, which you can remember as Every Guitarist Begins Doing Fine. The **spaces** are, (from bottom to top) F - A - C - E, which spells "Face."

LINES   E G B D F

SPACES   F A C E

The staff is divided into several parts by bar lines. The space between two bar lines is called a **measure** (also known as a "bar"). To end a piece of music a double bar is placed on the staff.

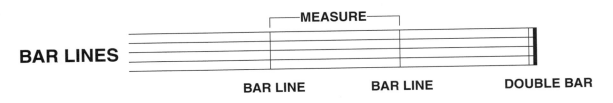

┌─── MEASURE ───┐

BAR LINES

BAR LINE   BAR LINE   DOUBLE BAR

Each measure contains a group of **beats**. Beats are the steady pulse of music. You respond to the pulse or beat when you tap your foot.

The two numbers placed next to the clef sign are the time signature.
The top number tells you how many beats are in one measure.

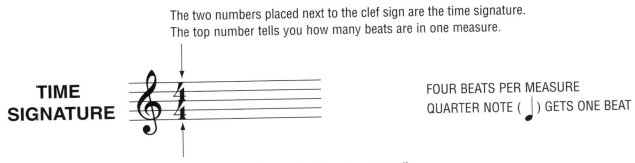

TIME SIGNATURE

FOUR BEATS PER MEASURE
QUARTER NOTE (♩) GETS ONE BEAT

The bottom number of the time signature tells you what kind of note will receive one beat.

Notes indicate the length (number of counts) of musical sound.

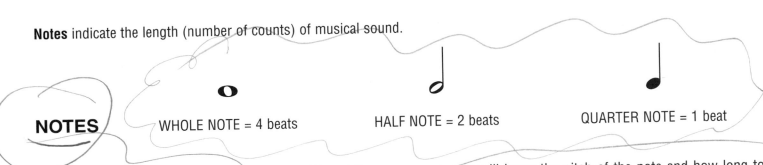

NOTES   WHOLE NOTE = 4 beats   HALF NOTE = 2 beats   QUARTER NOTE = 1 beat

When different kinds of notes are placed on different lines or spaces, you will know the pitch of the note and how long to play the sound.

NOTES ON THE FIRST STRING

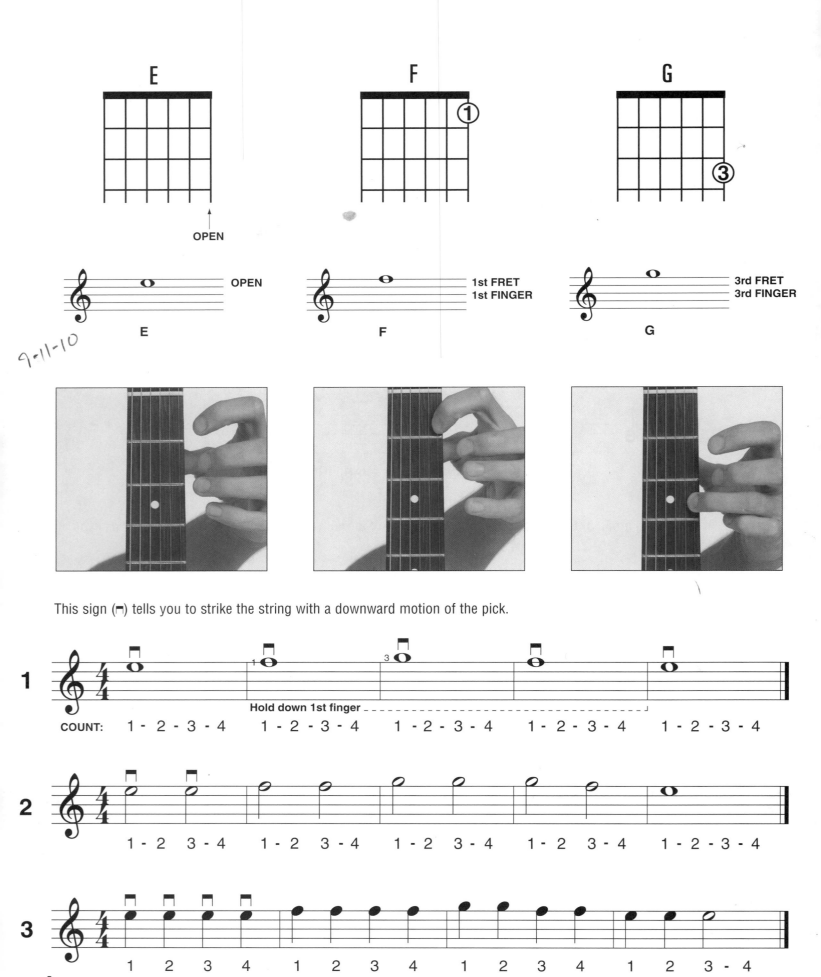

This sign (⊓) tells you to strike the string with a downward motion of the pick.

At first practice the exercises slowly and steadily. When you can play them well at a slow speed, gradually increase the tempo (speed).

Touch only the tips of the fingers on the strings.

Keep the left hand fingers arched over the strings.

Some songs are longer than one line. When you reach the end of the first line of music, continue on to the second line without stopping. Gray letters above the staff indicate chords to be played by your teacher. Measure numbers are given at the beginning of each new line of music.

GO ON TO THE NEXT LINE

SPANISH THEME

NOTES ON THE SECOND STRING

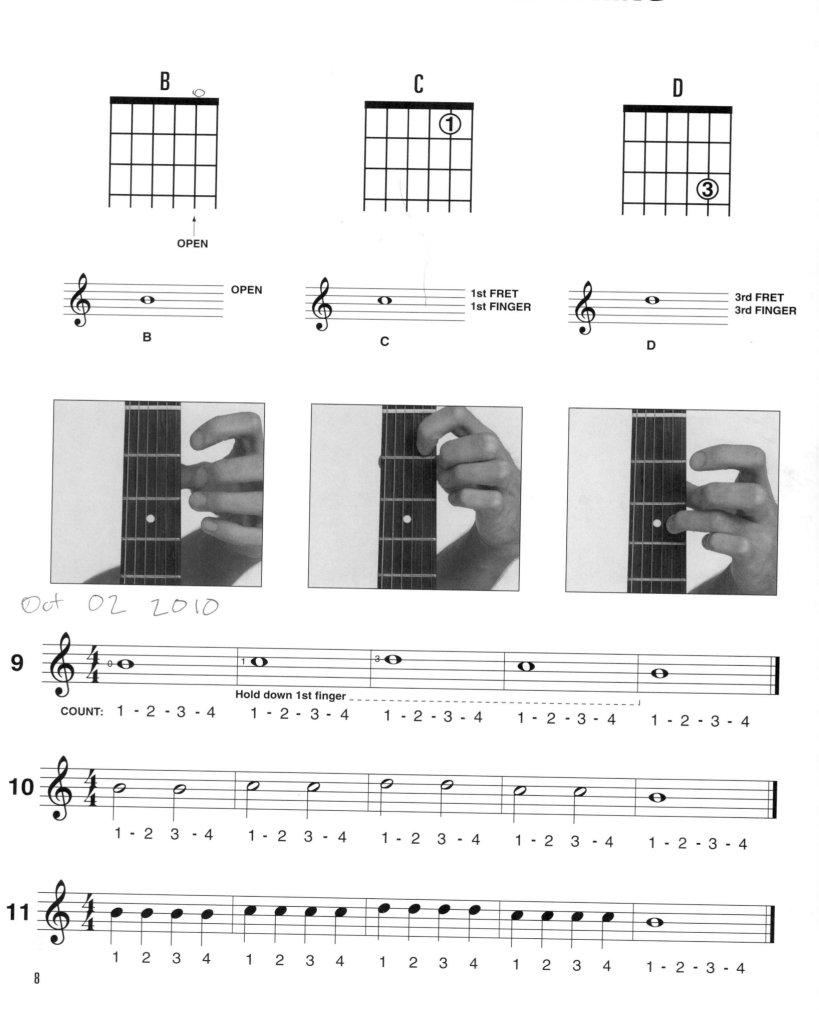

Oct 02 2010

9 COUNT: 1 - 2 - 3 - 4   1 - 2 - 3 - 4   1 - 2 - 3 - 4   1 - 2 - 3 - 4   1 - 2 - 3 - 4

Hold down 1st finger

10 1 - 2   3 - 4   1 - 2   3 - 4   1 - 2   3 - 4   1 - 2   3 - 4   1 - 2 - 3 - 4

11 1   2   3   4   1   2   3   4   1   2   3   4   1   2   3   4   1 - 2 - 3 - 4

Always practice the exercises slowly and steadily at first. After you can play them well at a slower tempo, gradually increase the speed. If some of your notes are fuzzy or unclear, move your left-hand finger slightly until you get a clear sound.

MOVING FROM STRING TO STRING

You have learned six notes now, three on the first string and three on the second string. In the following exercises you will be moving from string to string. As you are playing one note, look ahead to the next and get your fingers in position.

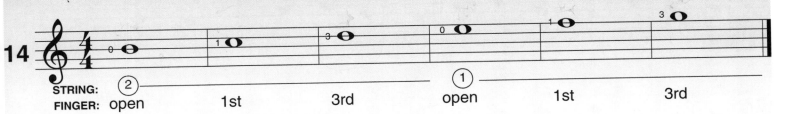

01-08 - 2011

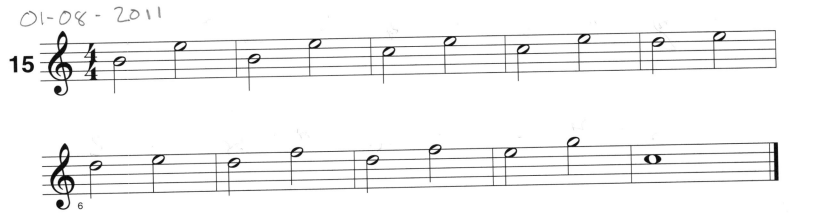

WORLD BEAT

9

Practice these songs played on strings 1 and 2. Always begin slowly and then gradually increase the tempo. Gray chord symbols are used throughout the book to indicate that the chords should be played by the instructor.

ODE TO JOY

Beethoven

NOTES ON THE THIRD STRING

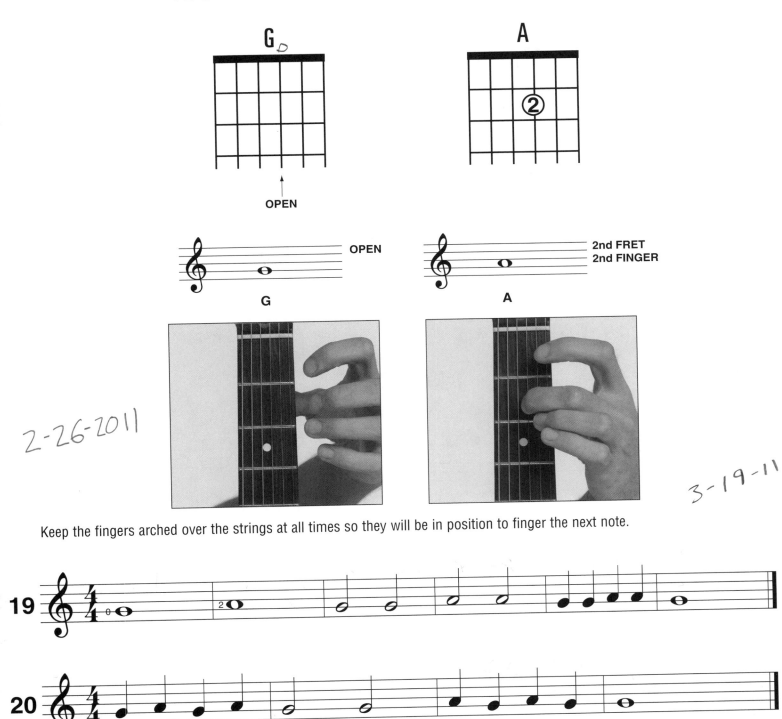

Keep the fingers arched over the strings at all times so they will be in position to finger the next note.

THREE-STRING REVIEW

Here are all the notes we've learned so far.

Play through these notes up and down. Then play just the. low G and the high G, and notice how similar they sound. The distance between two different notes with the same letter name is called an **octave**.

The following songs use notes on strings 1, 2, and 3.

ROCKIN' ROBIN

J. Thomas

03-26-2011

YANKEE DOODLE

Traditional

SURF ROCK

A **duet** is a song that has two parts that can be played together. Practice both parts of the following duet. Ask your instructor or a friend to play the duet with you.

AU CLAIR DE LA LUNE

France

AURA LEE

Poulton/Fosdick

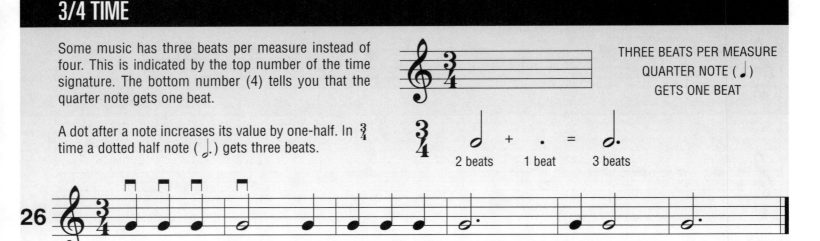

3/4 TIME

Some music has three beats per measure instead of four. This is indicated by the top number of the time signature. The bottom number (4) tells you that the quarter note gets one beat.

A dot after a note increases its value by one-half. In $\frac{3}{4}$ time a dotted half note (𝅗𝅥.) gets three beats.

THREE BEATS PER MEASURE
QUARTER NOTE (♩)
GETS ONE BEAT

$$\frac{3}{4} \quad \underset{\text{2 beats}}{𝅗𝅥} + \underset{\text{1 beat}}{.} = \underset{\text{3 beats}}{𝅗𝅥.}$$

COUNT: 1   2   3   1 - 2   3   1   2   3   1 - 2 - 3   1   2 - 3   1 - 2 - 3

HE'S A JOLLY GOOD FELLOW

England

NOTES ON THE FOURTH STRING

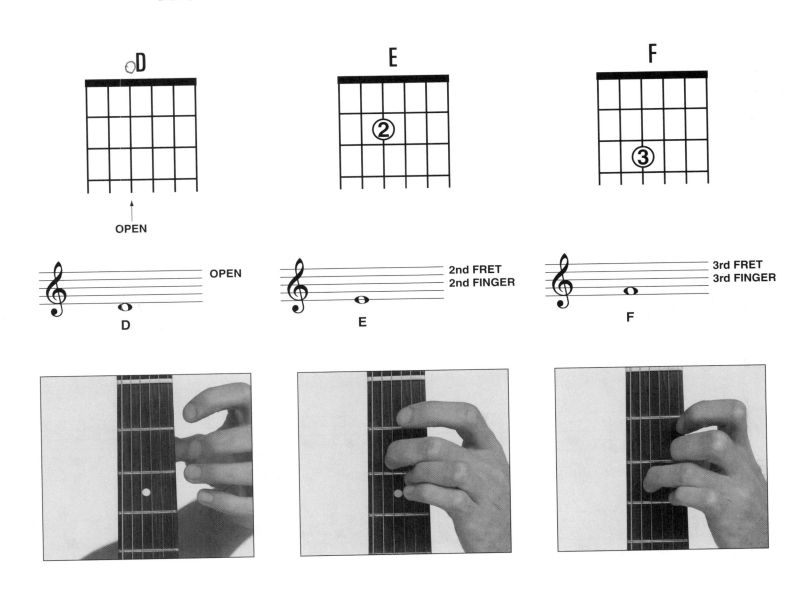

Practice each exercise carefully. Remember to keep your fingers arched over the strings.

PICKUP NOTES

Music doesn't always begin on beat one. When you begin after beat one, the notes before the first full measure are called **pickup notes**. Following are two examples of pickup notes. Count the missing beats out loud before you begin playing.

When a song begins with pickup notes, the last measure will be short the exact number of beats used as pickups.

WORRIED MAN BLUES

Traditional

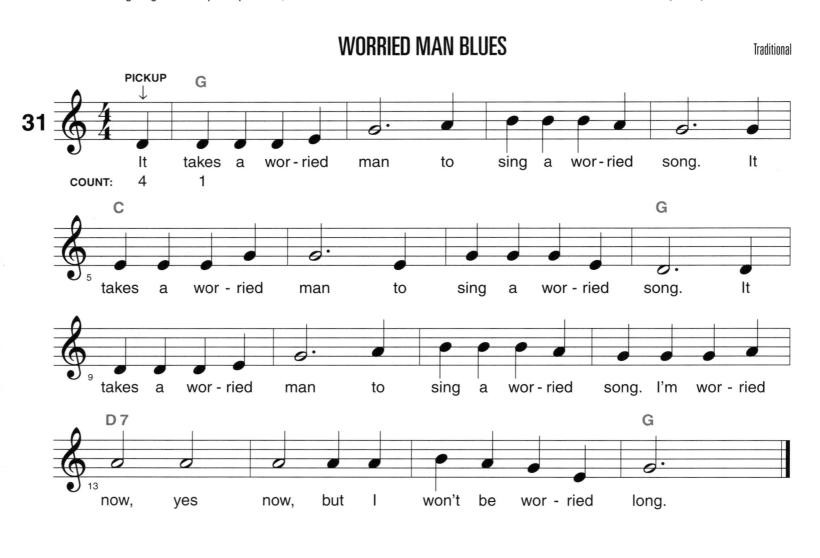

PLAYING CHORDS

A **chord** is sounded when more than two notes or strings are played at the same time. To begin you will be playing chords on three strings with only one finger depressed. Disregard the light gray finger numbers on strings 4, 5, and 6 until you can easily play the one-finger versions of the chords below.

The C Chord

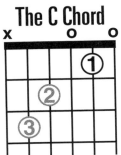

The G7 Chord

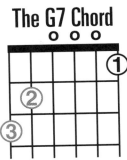

Study the illustrations for the chords above. An "o" above a string indicates that the string should be played "open" (not depressed by a finger). An "x" above a string indicates that the string should not be strummed. Refer to the hand positions in the photos below for additional visual guidance.

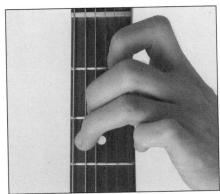
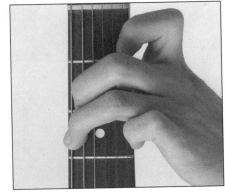

Depress the strings indicated with the tips of your fingers. Arch your fingers to avoid touching strings that are to be played open. Strum over the strings with a downward motion. All strings should sound as one, not separately.

Practice the following exercise strumming once for each slash mark. Keep a steady beat, and change chord fingerings quickly.

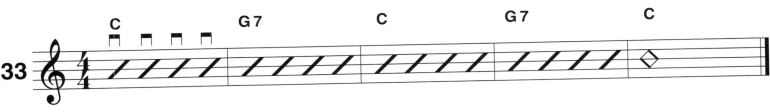

Now apply this strum to the song below.

TOM DOOLEY

Traditional

Next, let's try two more chords: G and D7. Notice that the G chord can be played two different ways.

The G Chord

The G Chord
(alternative fingering)

The D7 Chord

Strum once for each slash mark below.

35

G — D7

G — D7 — G — D7 — G

Review the fingering for the C chord and then practice Exercise 36 until you can play it well. Whenever you are moving between the C chord and the D7 chord, keep the first finger down.

36

G — C — D7 — G

PAY ME MY MONEY DOWN

Georgia Sea Islands

37

G — D7

Pay me, oh pay me, pay me my mon-ey down.

G

Pay me or go to jail, pay me my mon-ey down.

The following exercises use the four chords you have learned so far. The chords are arranged in sequences called **chord progressions**.

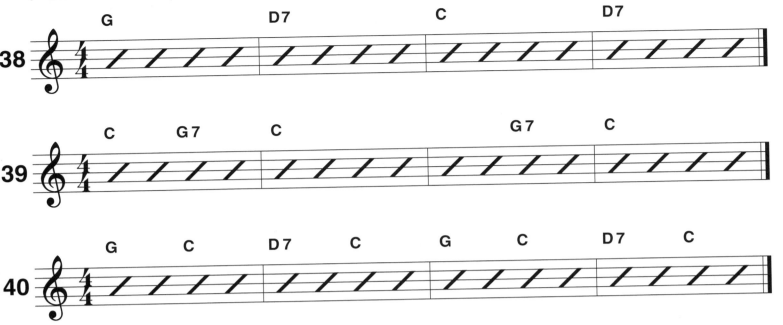

MOVING FROM CHORD TO CHORD

As you are playing one chord, look ahead to the next and get your fingers in position. Then, switch chords using a minimum of hand motion.

Trade off strumming the chords and playing the melody with your teacher or a friend.

12-BAR ROCK

You can also play the G, C, and D7 chords with "Worried Man Blues" on page 16.

TIES

A curved line which connects two notes of the same pitch is called a **tie**. The first note is struck and held for the value of both notes. The second note should not be played again. Look at the following example of tied notes.

Practice trading off on melody and chords in these pieces.

AMAZING GRACE

Traditional

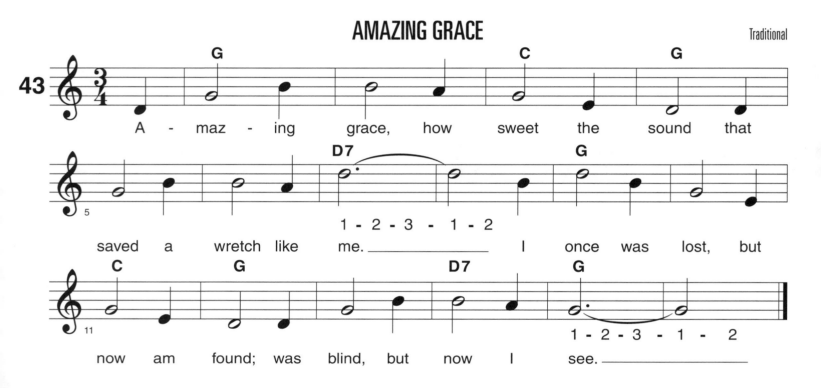

A - maz - ing   grace,   how   sweet   the   sound   that

saved   a   wretch   like   me. _____   I   once   was   lost,   but

now   am   found;   was   blind,   but   now   I   see. _____

RIFFIN'

WHEN THE SAINTS GO MARCHING IN

Traditional

WILL THE CIRCLE BE UNBROKEN

Country Gospel

NOTES ON THE FIFTH STRING

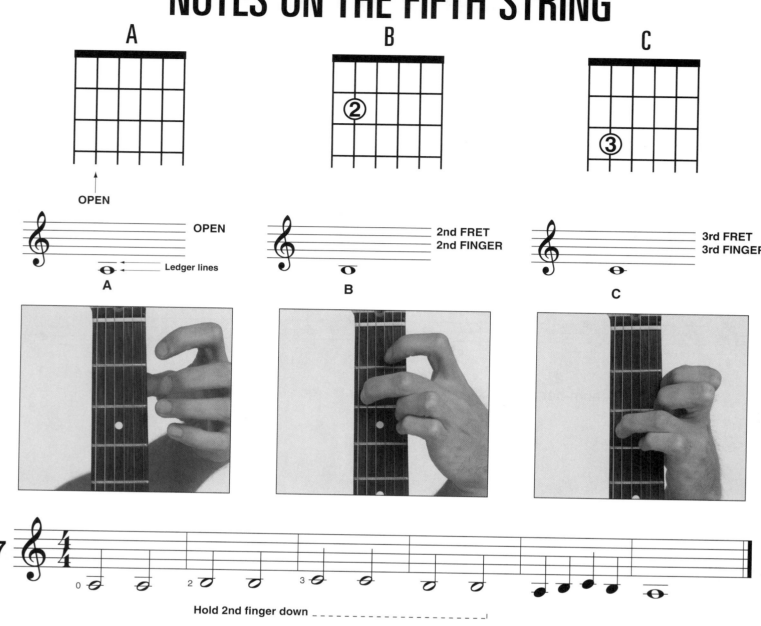

A

OPEN

OPEN

Ledger lines

A

B

2nd FRET
2nd FINGER

B

C

3rd FRET
3rd FINGER

C

47

Hold 2nd finger down _

BLUES BASS

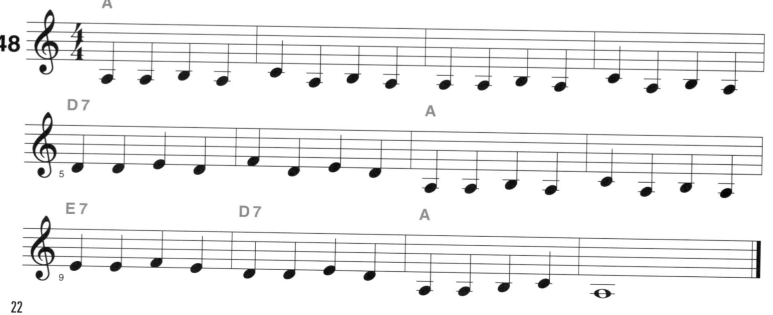

A

48

D 7

A

5

E 7

D 7

A

9

Practice these familiar melodies until you feel comfortable playing them. Remember to look ahead as you play so you can prepare for the next notes.

JOSHUA FOUGHT THE BATTLE OF JERICHO

Spiritual

GREENSLEEVES

England

NOTES ON THE SIXTH STRING

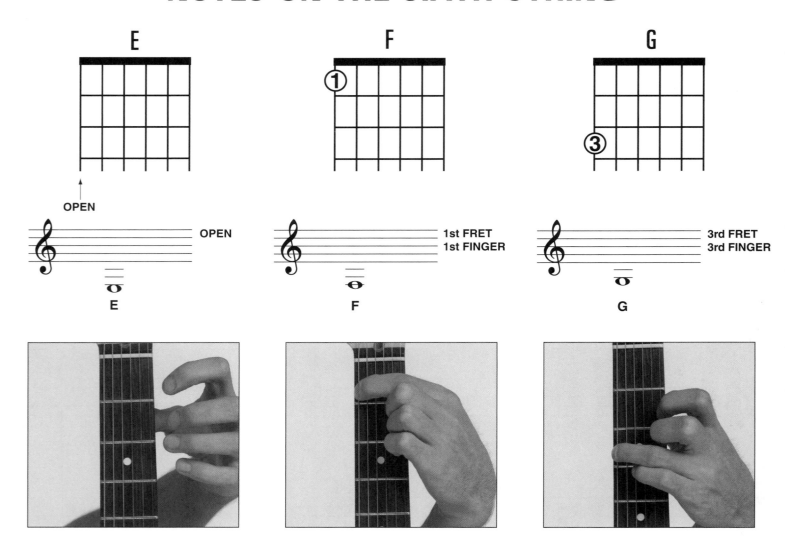

After you play these exercises, write the letter names below each note.

DOO-WOP

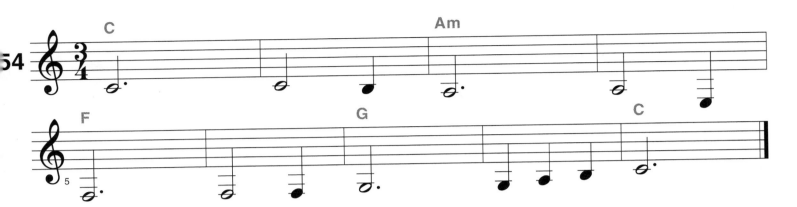

GIVE MY REGARDS TO BROADWAY

George M. Cohan

BASS ROCK

HALF AND WHOLE STEPS

The distance between music tones is measured by half steps and whole steps. On your guitar the distance between one fret and the next fret is a half step. The distance from one fret to the third fret in either direction is called a whole step.

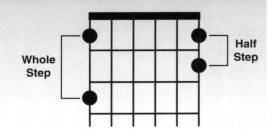

F-SHARP (F#)

When a **sharp** (#) is placed in front of a note, the note is raised a half step and played one fret higher. A sharp placed before a note affects all notes on the same line or space that follow in that measure. Following are the three F#s that appear on the fretboard to the right:

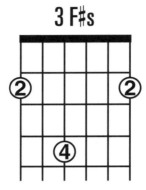

3 F#s

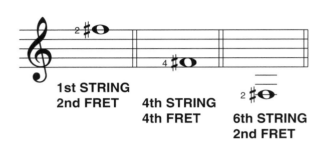

1st STRING
2nd FRET

4th STRING
4th FRET

6th STRING
2nd FRET

Practice each of these finger exercises many times.

57

DANNY BOY (LONDONDERRY AIR)

Ireland

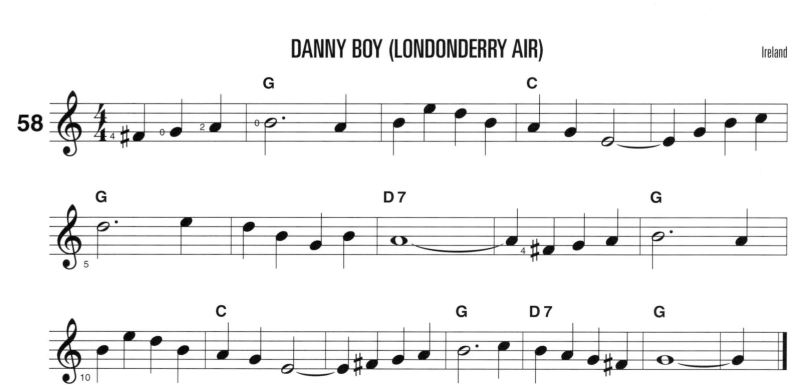

58

26

KEY SIGNATURES

Instead of writing a sharp sign before every F in a song, one sharp is placed at the beginning of the line. This is called a **key signature** and indicates that every F in the song should be played as F♯. In "Shenandoah" there will be an arrow above each F♯ to remind you to play F♯.

SHENANDOAH

Sea Shanty

Oh Shen - an - doah ____ I long to see you, ____ A -
way ____ you roll - ing riv - er, ____ Oh Shen - an - doah ____
____ I long to see you, ____ A - way ____ we're bound a -
way ____ a - cross the wide Miss - ou - ri. ____

SPY RIFF

RESTS

Musical **rests** are moments of silence in music. Each type of note has a matching rest which has the same name and receives the same number of counts.

Whole	Half	Quarter
4 beats	2 beats	1 beat

A rest often requires that you stop the sound of your guitar strings with your right hand as is shown in the photo to the right. This process is called **dampening** the strings. Use the edge of your right palm to touch the strings, and work for little unnecessary movement.

As you play the following exercises that contain both notes and rests, count aloud using numbers for the notes and say the word, "rest," for each beat of silence.

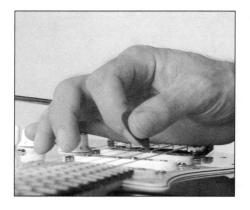

The letter **R** is used in place of the word "rest."

DEEP BLUE

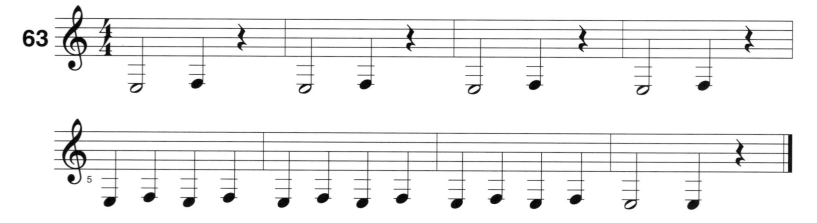

RED RIVER VALLEY

Cowboy Song

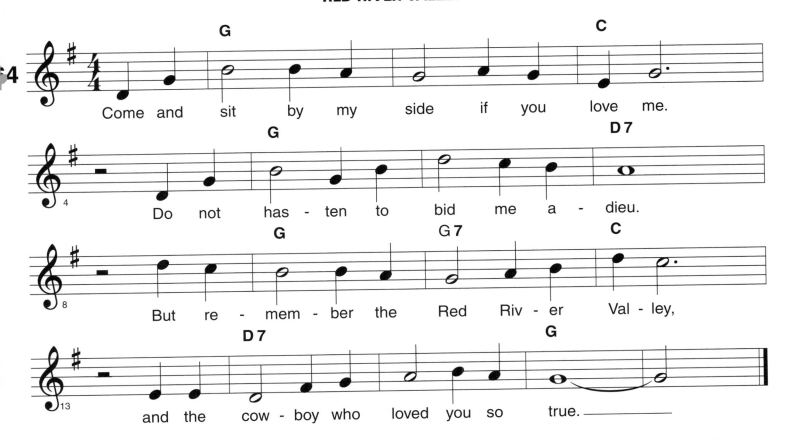

G ... **C**
Come and sit by my side if you love me.

G ... **D7**
Do not has - ten to bid me a - dieu.

G ... **G7** ... **C**
But re - mem - ber the Red Riv - er Val - ley,

D7 ... **G**
and the cow - boy who loved you so true. _____

TWANG

In ¾ a complete measure of rest (3 counts) is written as a whole rest (▬).

ROCK 'N' REST

EIGHTH NOTES

An **eighth note** is half the length of a quarter note and receives half a beat in $\frac{4}{4}$ or $\frac{3}{4}$ meter.

One eighth note is written with a flag. Consecutive eighth notes are connected with a beam.

To count eighth notes, divide the beat into two, and use "and" between the beats. Count the measure to the right aloud while tapping your foot on the beat.

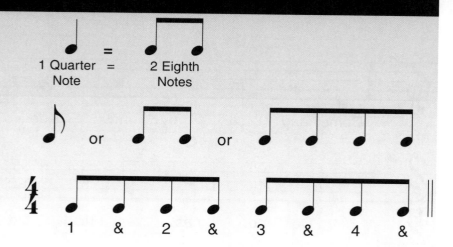

Eighth notes are played with a **downstroke** (⊓) of the pick on the beat and an **upstroke** (∨) on the "and." This is called **alternate picking**.

Playing the following exercise using alternate picking for all eighth notes and strictly downstrokes for all quarter notes. Practice slowly and steadily at first; then gradually increase the speed.

A double bar with two dots (:|) is a **repeat sign**, and it tells you to play the music a second time.

SEA SHANTY

FRÉRE JACQUES

France

Fré - re   Jac - ques,   Fré - re   Jac - ques,   dor - mez vous?   Dor - mez vous?
Are you sleep - ing?   Are you sleep - ing?   Broth - er   John,   Broth - er   John,

Son - nez les ma - tin - es,   son - nez les ma - tin - es,   din, din, don;   din, din, don.
Morn - ing bells are ring - ing,   morn - ing bells are ring - ing,   ding, dong, ding;   ding, dong, ding.

SNAKE CHARMER

Try playing "Snake Charmer" again, this time on the higher strings. Begin an octave higher with the A note on the second fret of the third string, and use your ear as a guide.

THE STAR-SPANGLED BANNER

Key/Smith

MORE STRUMMING

The alternating down-up stroke pattern you have already played on eighth notes can also be applied to strumming. As you practice the following exercise, keep you wrist relaxed and flexible. The down-up motion will be much faster and easier if you use motion of the wrist only, rather than of the entire arm. This wrist motion feels a little like shaking water off the hand.

BASIC DOWN-UP STRUM

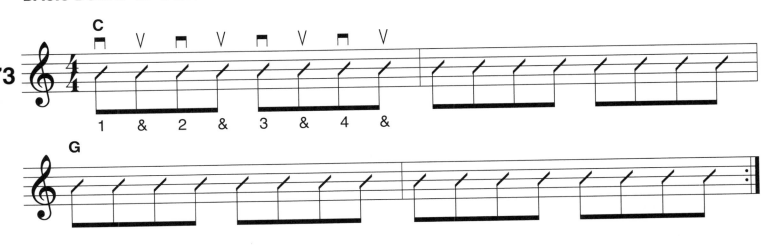

STRUM VARIATIONS

A variation of the basic down-up strum misses the upstroke or "and" of the first beat. Remember to keep the down-up motion going and miss the strings on the "and" of beat one.

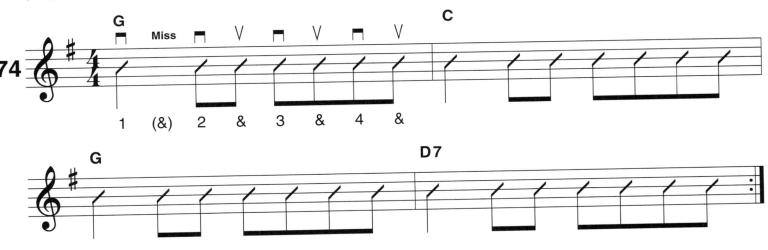

This variation misses two upstrokes. Continue to strum but miss the strings on the "and" of beats one and three.

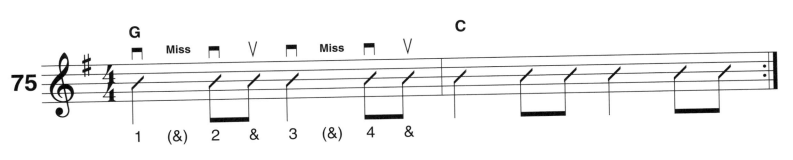

THE Em CHORD

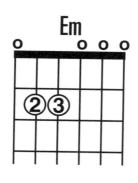

The E minor chord is one of the easiest chords on the guitar. Arch your fingers and play on the tips to avoid touching the other open strings.

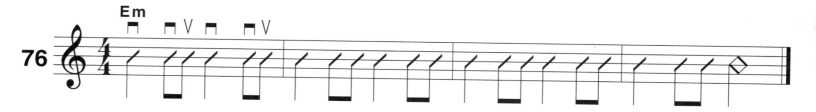

HEY, HO, NOBODY HOME

England

Hey, ho, no - bod - y home. Meat, nor drink, nor

mon - ey have I none, yet will I be mer - ry. (ry.)

SHALOM CHAVERIM
(Peace, My Friend)

Israel

Sha - lom, cha - ve - rim! Sha - lom, cha - ve - rim! Sha - lom, sha -

lom! Le - hit - ra - ot, le - hit - ra - ot. Sha - lom, sha - lom.

CHORD PAIRS

As you move between different chords, if one or more fingers remain on the same note, allow them to stay pressed as you switch chords. In the following progression there is a common finger between the G and Em chords and a common finger between the C and D7 chords.

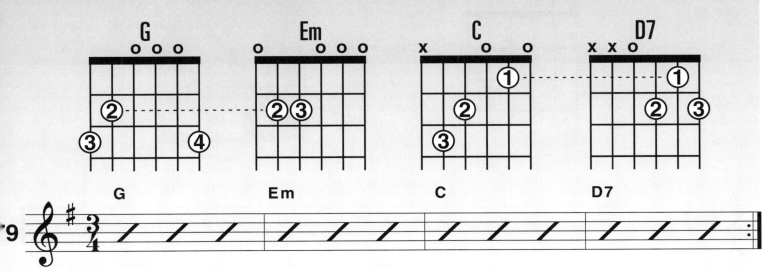

Practice the following chord progressions until you can play them steadily and without any hesitation between chord changes. Try to move your fingers to a new chord as a unit instead of "letting your fingers do the walking" one at a time.

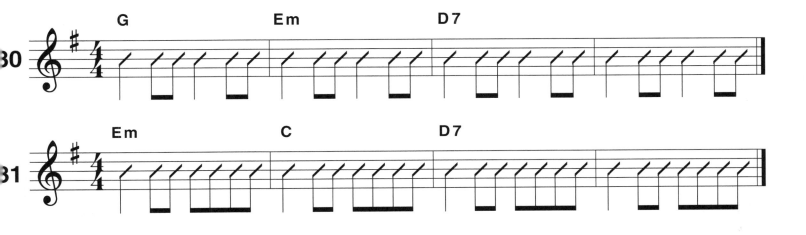

You can vary the strumming by alternating between a bass note (usually the lowest note of a chord and the name of the chord) and the remainder of the chord. This style of accompaniment is referred to as the **bass note strum**, or "boom chick" rhythm.

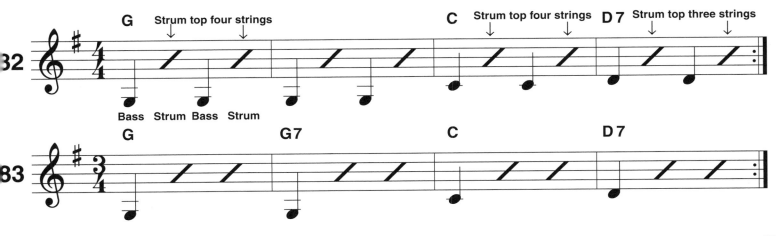

THE D CHORD

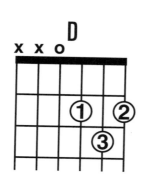

84 Em / D / C / D

85 Em / D C / Em / D C

THIS TRAIN

African American

86 G
This train is bound for glo-ry, this train. ____

D
This train is bound for glo-ry, this train. ____

G   G7   C   G   D
This train is bound for glo-ry, if you want to ride it you must be ho-ly.

G   D   G
This train is bound for glo-ry, this train. ____

BOOGIE BASS

The next example uses a variation on the bass note strum technique. This time, strike the bass note and then strum the remainder of the chord twice.

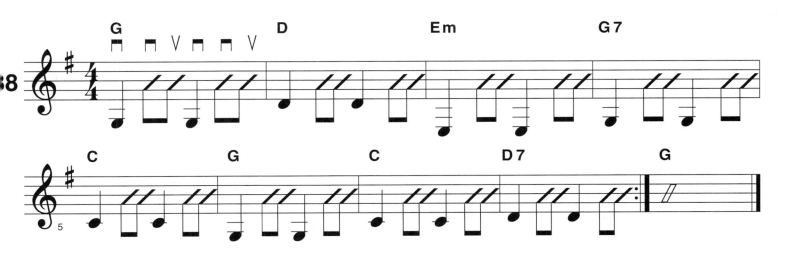

Practice these strums before playing "Simple Gifts."

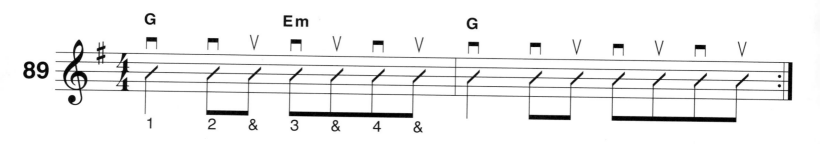

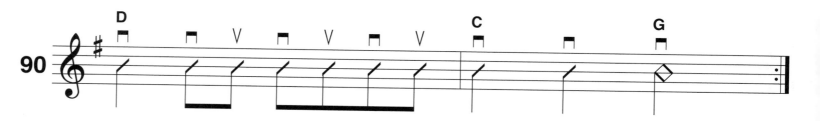

On "Simple Gifts" you can play the melody (Part 1), the harmony line (Part 2), or the chordal accompaniment.

SIMPLE GIFTS

Shaker Song

C-SHARP (C#)

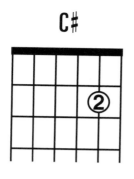

C#

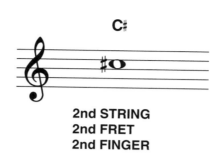

C#

2nd STRING
2nd FRET
2nd FINGER

92

93

ROCKIN' BLUES

A7

D7   A7

E7   D7   A7

THE A7 CHORD

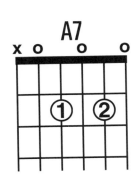

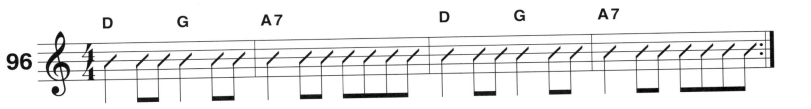

DOWN IN THE VALLEY

Traditional

MINUET IN G

J.S. BACH

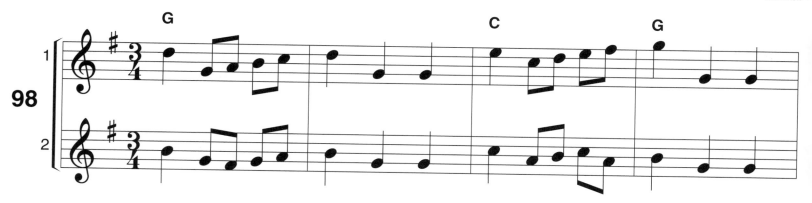

98

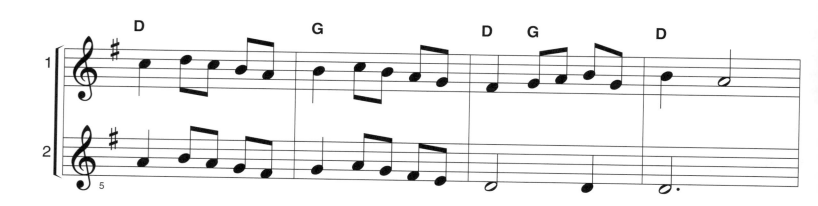

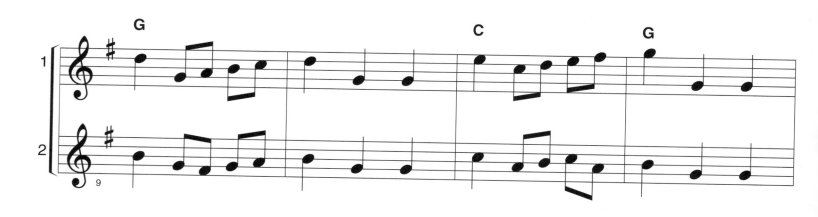

Repeat to
top of page

TIME IS ON MY SIDE

Jerry Ragovoy

GRAND FINALE

CHORD CHART

In this chart you will find the chords learned in this book as well as several other common chords you may see in music you are playing.

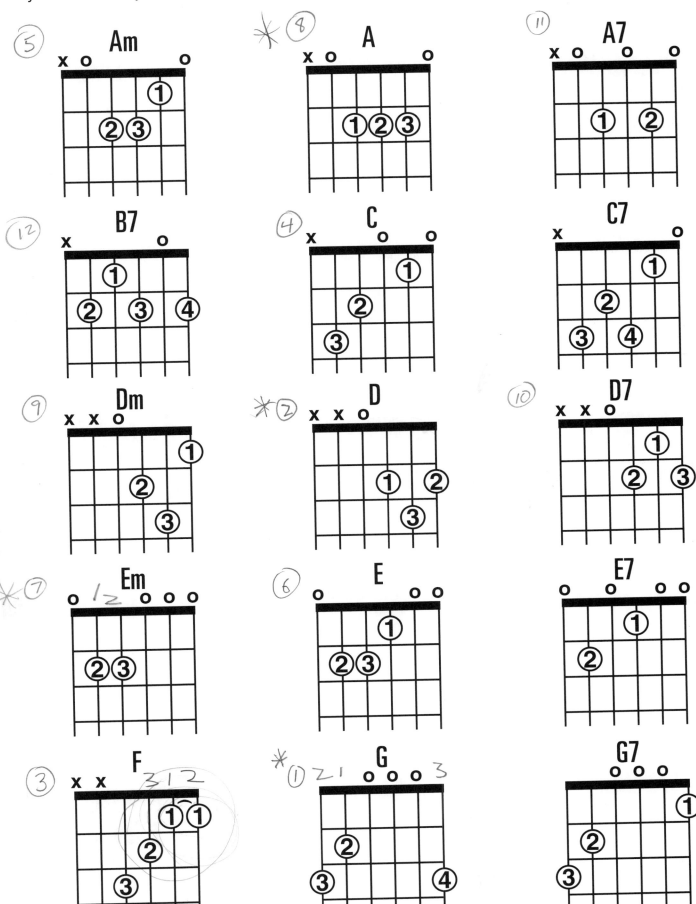